Mr Kiwi
has an important job

Words and pictures by Heather Hunt

potton & burton

Mr Kiwi has an important job because

Mrs Kiwi is his mate.

Mrs Kiwi gets to work.

She eats and eats

and eats and EATS!

Mr Kiwi waits.

Mr Kiwi must prepare.

He uses poo to mark his place

and kicks and claws to keep it safe.

He fills his tummy with bugs
and grubs and wriggly worms.

Mr Kiwi has an important job.

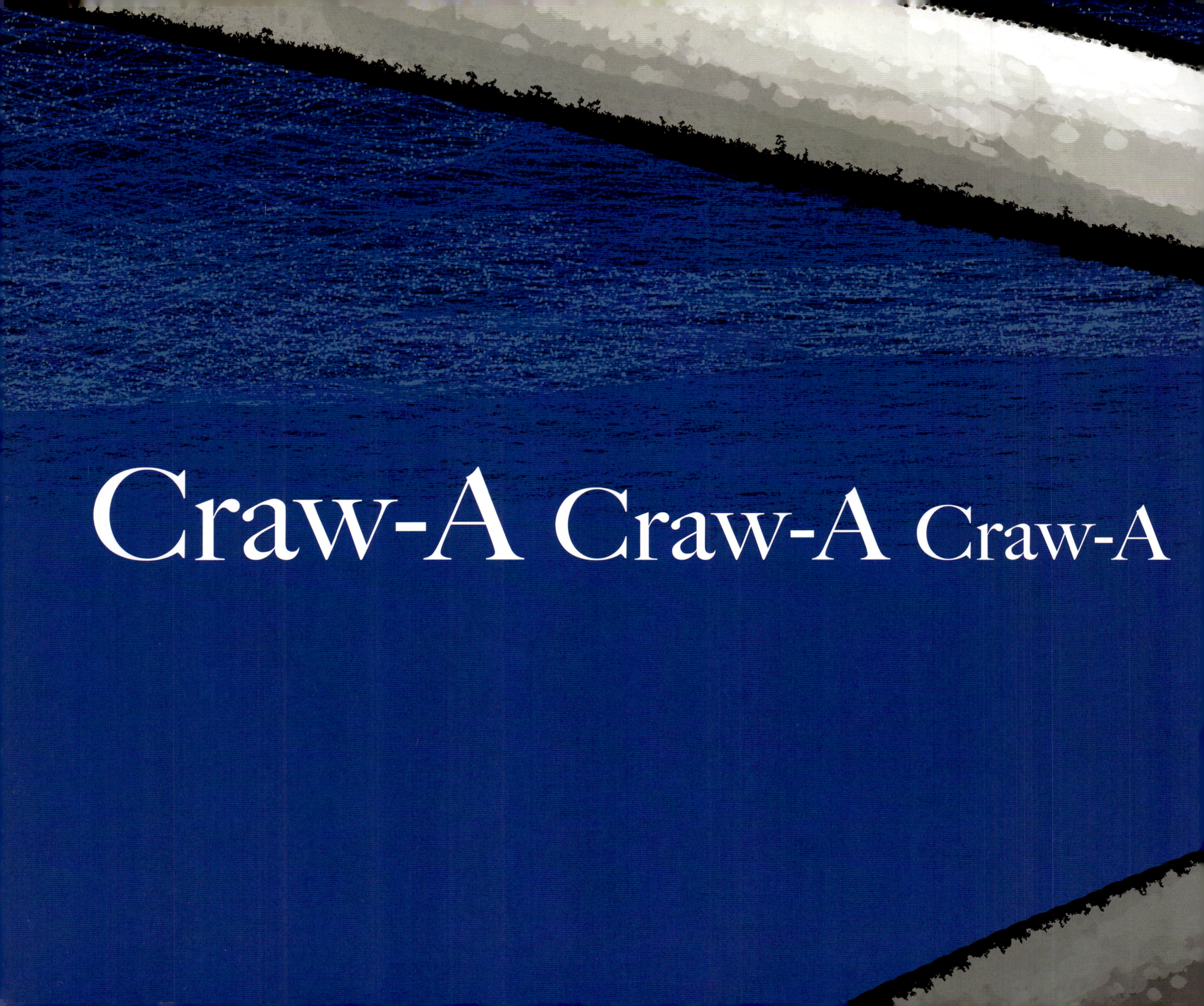
Craw-A Craw-A Craw-A

Craw-A Craw-A

Wait!

Is that his mate?

Mr Kiwi has an important job.

Mr Kiwi cannot be late!

Mrs Kiwi's work is done.

She goes away to feed and rest

while Mr Kiwi sits and nests.

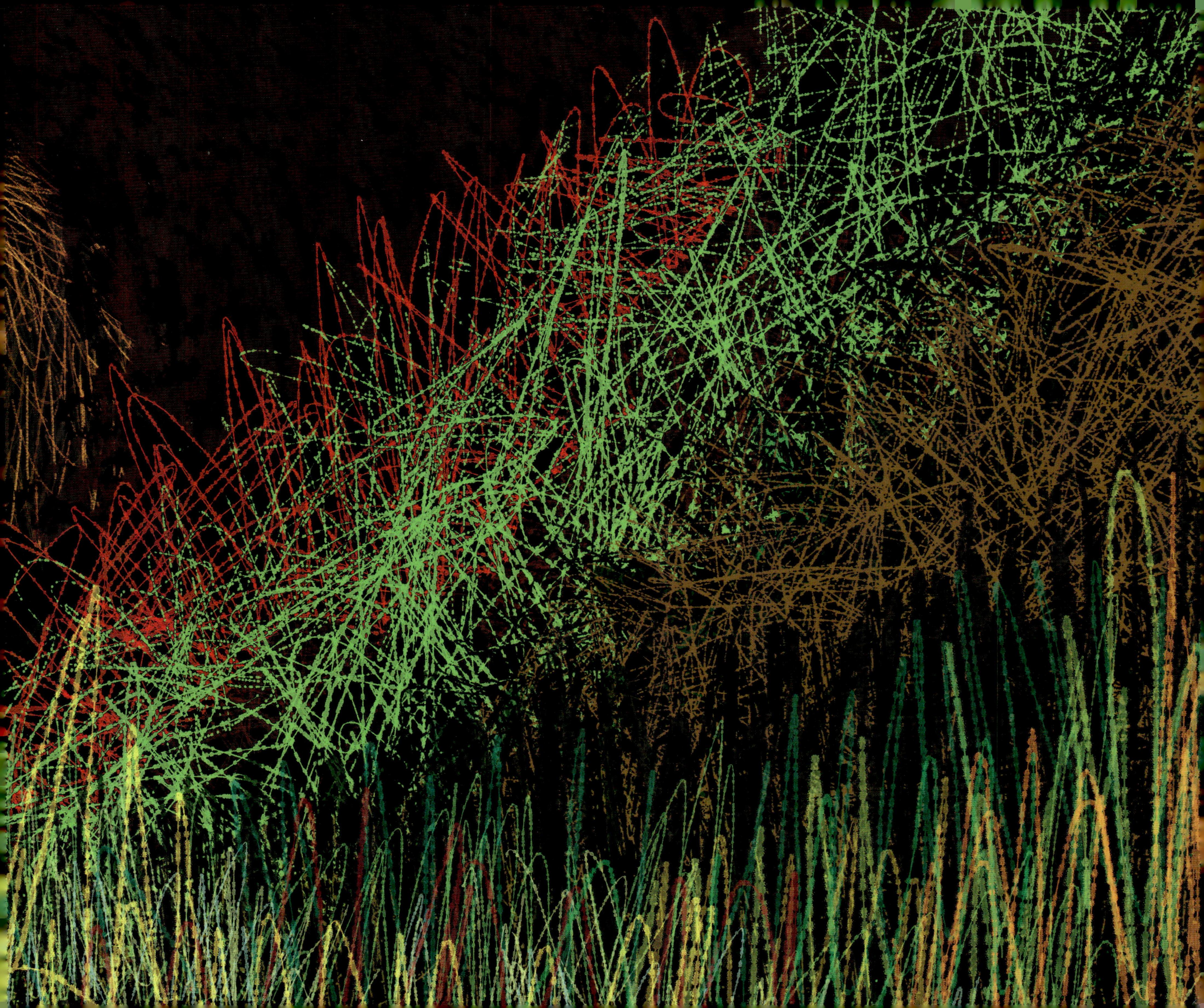

Wrapped around and snuggled down,

for eighty days

and eighty nights,

until the eggs begin to
CRACK...

and two young chicks are safely hatched!

'A picture book for me is a treasure, something to behold, something to share and something to return to again and again. I loved writing and illustrating *Mr Kiwi* and wish to thank Barbara Else for challenging my thinking, and Robbie Burton for his enthusiasm and endorsement.'
– Heather

Heather's involvement with Backyard Kiwi (a kiwi recovery project) provides a rich source of kiwi stories and has inspired three award-winning picture books, ***It's my egg (and you can't have it!)***, ***The Cuckoo and the Warbler***, and ***KIWI the real story***.

First published in 2019 by Potton & Burton
319 Hardy Street, PO Box 221
Nelson, New Zealand
pottonandburton.co.nz

Artwork and text © Heather Hunt
Paperback ISBN 978 1 98 855004 6
Hardback ISBN 978 1 98 855005 3

Printed in China by
Midas Printing International Ltd